FROM EMPLOYEE TO ENTREPRENEUR

Developing the mindset and skills
for entrepreneurial success

By

Maxen Faisal

TABLE OF CONTENTS

INTRODUCTION:
CHAPTER 1:
THE CHANGE IN PERSPECTIVE
CHAPTER 2:
UNCOVERING YOUR ENTREPRENEURIAL PASSION
CHAPTER 3:
TRANSFORMING IDEAS INTO BUSINESS PLANS
CHAPTER 4:
FINANCIAL FOUNDATIONS
CHAPTER 5:
LEGAL CONSIDERATIONS
CHAPTER 6.
THE LAUNCH PHASE
CHAPTER 7:
MANAGING THE TRANSITION
CHAPTER 8
BUILDING YOUR ENTREPRENEURIAL TEAM
CHAPTER 9.
GROWTH AND SCALING STRATEGIES
CHAPTER 10:
NAVIGATING ENTREPRENEURIAL CHALLENGES
CHAPTER 11
CONNECTING AND FOSTERING CONNECTIONS
CHAPTER 12:
TRACKING   ACHIEVEMENTS   AND   ESTABLISHING
FRESH OBJECTIVES
CHAPTER 13:CONTINUING AND DEVELOPING YOUR
ENTREPRENEURIAL JOURNEY
CONCLUSION:
YOUR ENTREPRENEURIAL LEGACY

INTRODUCTION:

THE ENTREPRENEURIAL AWAKENING

In the world of careers and dreams, there is a crucial juncture for some—a sudden realization, a silent inner voice, or maybe an irresistible summons.

The time one realizes the desire to transition from employee to entrepreneur.

Our journey starts by acknowledging 'The Entrepreneurial Awakening.'

Identifying the Entrepreneurial Urge

Entrepreneurship beckons to many as a quiet hunch, rather than a bold declaration.

Possible signs include discontentment with the present, longing for artistic independence, or a wish to create a greater influence on society.

Here, we explore the signs and signals of entrepreneurship.

We uncover employees' latent dreams and aspirations, poised to stir at the opportune time.

Navigating the Employee-to-Entrepreneur Transition

Moving from a stable job to entrepreneurship requires careful consideration.

It's a path of unknowns, finding yourself, and ongoing education.

This section acts as your guiding compass, leading you through the complexities of this important transition.
We'll cover the emotional, financial, and practical aspects of a smooth transition.

Overview of the Book

"The Entrepreneurial Awakening" is a complete roadmap for transforming your career and life, not just a simple guide.
The book is split into chapters that cover key topics for your transformation from employee to entrepreneur.
We will address mindset shifts, idea generation, business planning, financial readiness, legal considerations, launching your venture, and sustaining your entrepreneurial journey.
We'll guide you through every step of becoming a successful entrepreneur – from finding your passion to forming a strong team and measuring your achievements.

CHAPTER 1:

THE CHANGE IN PERSPECTIVE

Understanding the Employee Mindset

Prior to fully engaging in entrepreneurship, it is vital to grasp the employee mindset, which many of us hold in our careers.

You've spent countless years conforming to rules and guidelines in a structured environment, possibly for decades.

We will analyze the intricacies of the employee mindset, which includes job security, steady pay, and associated expectations and limitations.

Cultivating the Entrepreneurial Mindset

Entrepreneurship requires a mindset shift, transitioning from the familiar to the unfamiliar. Embrace the entrepreneurial mindset, breaking free from conventional boundaries.
Here, we examine the mindset's defining traits—initiative, risk-taking, innovation, and resilience.
We'll explore developing and enhancing these traits within oneself, as they can be improved and mastered like any other skill.

Embracing Change and Uncertainty

Entrepreneurship is constantly accompanied by change, and uncertainty often becomes its closest ally.

You'll experience doubt, fear, and discomfort when transitioning from the predictable employee's world to the ambiguous entrepreneur's world.

But, these moments also present enormous opportunities for growth.

We'll provide you with tools to excel amid change and uncertainty.

Embark on a transformative transition from employee to entrepreneur.

It's an experience that will test, inspire, and ultimately reshape your perspective on your career and your life.

Mindset shifts often initiate significant transformations, so remember this as you start this new chapter.

CHAPTER 2:

UNCOVERING YOUR ENTREPRENEURIAL PASSION

Discovering Your Hobbies and Engagements

Passion drives successful entrepreneurs through challenges.

In this chapter, we'll explore ourselves.

We'll discover what you love and what makes you happy.

Discover business ideas that truly resonate with your passions by exploring your interests.

Identifying Potential Business Ideas

Businesses begin with ideas, but not all ideas are alike.

We will help you identify and evaluate potential business ideas.

We will explore methods for generating and honing ideas that are in line with your passions, skills, and objectives.

This chapter will provide you with viable business ideas to explore.

Aligning Passion with Opportunity

Success in entrepreneurship is achieved by combining your passion with a viable market opportunity.

It's the point where your enthusiasm aligns with your target audience's needs and desires.

We'll instruct you on market assessment, gap identification, and aligning business ideas with authentic opportunities.

You'll create a profitable and sustainable business by following this approach.

Remember, your entrepreneurial journey starts with a passion-aligned idea sparked as you progress through this chapter.

This chapter will help you ignite and transform your spark into an entrepreneurial flame.

CHAPTER 3:

TRANSFORMING IDEAS INTO BUSINESS PLANS

Developing Your Business Concept

You've discovered a valuable idea that aligns with your passions and market opportunities.

It is now time to shape that idea into a viable business plan.

In this section, we'll examine how to develop your idea, determine your product or service, and pinpoint your unique value proposition.

You'll discover how to define your vision and establish the foundation for your entrepreneurial path.

Developing an Effective Business Plan

A well-crafted business plan ensures your venture's success.
It's both a funding securement document and a guiding roadmap.
We'll explore key components of a successful business plan, including market analysis and financial projections.
You'll develop a plan that aligns with your vision and aids in decision-making and growth.

Assessing Idea Feasibility

Realism is crucial, even when accompanied by passion and enthusiasm.
In this part, we will guide you on evaluating the viability of your business concept.

We'll examine market demand, competition, regulations, and financial viability.

You'll have the tools to decide if your idea is worth pursuing by the end of this chapter.

Upon exploring this chapter, keep in mind that the process of moving from an idea to a business plan is when your entrepreneurial aspirations begin to materialize.

It is a vital stage that establishes the foundation for your venture's success.

Approach it with dedication and passion, and you'll be on track to turning your idea into a successful enterprise.

CHAPTER 4:

FINANCIAL FOUNDATIONS

Assessing Your Financial Situation

Assess your finances before starting your entrepreneurial journey.

We'll assess your personal finances thoroughly in this section.

You will discover how to compute your present net value, grasp your money inflow, and recognize any current financial obligations or limitations.

This self-reflection will reveal your financial baseline.

Creating a Startup Budget

A well-organized budget is crucial for effectively managing the finances of your business.

We'll cover the startup budget process, which includes estimating costs, expenses, and revenue projections.

You'll develop skills to establish attainable financial objectives and effectively manage available resources.

You'll have a practical budget for your early stages as an entrepreneur by the end of this section.

Funding Your Entrepreneurial Venture

Obtain the required financing after evaluating your finances and creating a budget to launch your business.

We'll explore funding choices for entrepreneurs, ranging from bootstrapping and personal savings to loans, grants, and investors.
You'll understand the pros and cons of each funding source and make informed decisions based on your business' needs.

Financial preparedness is important when transitioning from employee to entrepreneur.
Understanding your financial landscape is vital for informed decision-making and ensuring the sustainability of your business.

CHAPTER 5:

LEGAL CONSIDERATIONS

Business Legal Structures

The legal structure you choose for your business affects taxes and liability, so it's a crucial decision.
We'll cover different legal structures: sole proprietorships, partnerships, LLCs, and corporations.

You'll obtain insights on advantages and disadvantages of each structure, aiding in an informed choice aligned with your business goals.

Business Registration and Licensing

Register and license your business after choosing a legal structure.
We'll guide you through the required steps, paperwork, and government entities for registration.
You'll discover how to comply with the unique legal regulations in your area and sector, preventing legal risks and maintaining a compliant business.

Contractual and legal obligations regarding intellectual property

Adhering to legal regulations is vital for safeguarding your business as contracts underpin all business transactions.

This section explores contracts, covering essentials, negotiation strategies, and common types.

We will also discuss the significance of protecting your intellectual property such as patents, trademarks, and copyrights, to safeguard your distinct concepts and assets.

Understanding the legal aspects of entrepreneurship is vital for establishing a strong foundation for your venture, even though it may seem complicated.

Ensure compliance and protect your interests by understanding legal structures, completing registrations, and safeguarding intellectual property.

CHAPTER 6.

THE LAUNCH PHASE

Preparing for Business Launch

Your entrepreneurial venture is about to launch—the moment you've been working towards.
Before leaping, be prepared.
We'll help you prepare for a successful business launch.

We'll address product finalization, establishing your physical or online presence, and organizing essential logistics.

You'll be ready for your business debut by the end of this section.

Marketing and Branding Strategies

Making your business available is important, but so is making it known.

We'll explore specific marketing and branding tactics to match your distinct business identity.

You'll learn how to effectively connect with and captivate your desired audience through brand storytelling and strategic marketing strategies.

This section will help you build a powerful brand presence and generate buzz for your launch.

Beginning and Early Obstacles

Entrepreneurship's beginning entails both excitement and challenge.

Discover the essential actions to take after launching your business, such as acquiring customers and the significance of fostering relationships.

You'll also gain skills in overcoming challenges that arise, such as handling cash flow and resolving unforeseen issues.

You'll feel confident to start your journey as an entrepreneur when you finish this chapter.

The launch phase is where your vision becomes reality.

Take action, demonstrate your passion, and confront the challenges.

Embrace this stage resolutely for a solid entrepreneurial start.

CHAPTER 7:

MANAGING THE TRANSITION

Juggling Employee Obligations and Entrepreneurial Responsibilities

The transition from employee to entrepreneur is typically a gradual process, not an abrupt jump.
During this transition, you may need to balance your current job and the needs of your new business.
We'll discuss methods to effectively balance these responsibilities, such as time management tactics and establishing boundaries to safeguard

your professional career and entrepreneurial aspirations.

Managing Feelings during Change

Even chosen change can be emotionally difficult.
We'll explore the emotional aspects of going from employee to entrepreneur in this section.
We'll cover typical emotional obstacles: fear, self-doubt, and the discomfort of leaving your comfort zone.
You'll gain techniques to handle these emotions and maintain resilience during the transition.

Time Management and Productivity

Time is precious as you manage your work and entrepreneurial pursuit.

Time management and productivity are crucial for success.

We'll offer practical advice and resources to help you make the most of your time, including task prioritization and distraction reduction.

By the chapter's end, you'll optimize your time during this phase.

Note the careful balancing act required when transitioning from employee to entrepreneur as you engage with this chapter.

It necessitates a combination of practicality, emotional intelligence, and skillful time management.

By mastering this phase, you'll make your transition into full-time entrepreneurship smoother.

CHAPTER 8

BUILDING YOUR ENTREPRENEURIAL TEAM

The Significance of a Supportive Network

Collaboration and support are crucial for entrepreneurship; it is not a solo effort.

We'll stress the need for a strong support system in this section.

You'll discover how to find and build relationships with mentors, advisors, and fellow entrepreneurs who can provide guidance, insights, and support.

A robust network can support your entrepreneurial journey and offer security when faced with difficulties.

Engaging and Coordinating with Allies

You may need assistance as your business expands.

Partner with like-minded individuals or organizations to expand your vision and enhance your abilities.

We will assist you in identifying potential partners, conducting effective interviews, and establishing mutually beneficial collaborations.

Discover the secrets of creating a goal-oriented and value-based team.

Leadership and Management for Effective Teams

Being an entrepreneur often entails being a leader.

Assessing leadership attributes and abilities within the entrepreneurial realm.

You'll acquire skills in leading by example, effectively communicating your vision, and motivating your team.

We'll also explore team management practically, covering delegation, conflict resolution, and building a positive work culture.

By this chapter's end, you'll be capable of successfully leading and managing your entrepreneurial team.

CHAPTER 9

GROWTH AND SCALING STRATEGIES

Ensuring Long-Term Success by Scaling Your Business

Once your business gains momentum, scaling is the obvious next move for lasting prosperity.
We will examine scaling, a deliberate and strategic process for business growth without compromising core values and quality.
You'll discover ways to expand, such as by boosting production, entering fresh markets, or diversifying your product range.

Strategies for Sustainable Growth

Sustainable growth encompasses both expansion and the ability to thrive in the long run.

We'll discuss ways to achieve sustainable growth, such as retaining customers, fostering innovation, and ensuring financial stability.

Maintain business resilience and adaptability by finding the optimal growth-stability equilibrium.

Overcoming Scaling Challenges

Scaling a business comes with challenges like handling increased demand and ensuring product/service quality.

We'll explore typical obstacles entrepreneurs encounter while scaling and offer strategies for conquering them.

You'll learn strategies to handle resource constraints, organizational changes, and the need for efficient systems and processes.

CHAPTER 10:

NAVIGATING ENTREPRENEURIAL CHALLENGES

Entrepreneurs' Typical Obstacles

Entrepreneurship is a path filled with both opportunities and challenges.

In this section, we\'ll examine some of the common challenges that entrepreneurs encounter along their journey.

We will explore financial challenges, market changes, competitors, and decision-making pressures.

By grasping these challenges, you'll be more equipped to confront them directly.

Building Resilience and Adaptability

The ability to bounce back and adjust is key for entrepreneurs to navigate challenges and capitalize on opportunities.
We'll cover methods for developing resilience, such as stress and setback management techniques.
We'll also highlight adaptability, which involves pivoting, innovating, and learning from experiences.
You'll acquire essential qualities to prosper as an entrepreneur.

Transforming setbacks into opportunities for growth.

Failures and setbacks are valuable learning experiences in the entrepreneurial journey.

We will explore addressing setbacks with a growth mindset, gleaning insights and lessons from obstacles.

Learn how to turn setbacks into stepping stones for success and create a culture of continuous improvement and innovation in your entrepreneurial pursuits.

CHAPTER 11

CONNECTING AND FOSTERING CONNECTIONS

The Importance of Networking for Entrepreneurs

Entrepreneurs benefit from networking, which facilitates growth, collaboration, and support.
Here, we'll examine networking's inherent value.
Building a strong network offers insights, opens doors, and creates a sense of community.
We'll explore networking strategies and the advantages of connecting with fellow

entrepreneurs, industry professionals, and potential mentors.

Building Authentic Business Relationships

Authenticity is crucial in entrepreneurship relationships.
We'll explore the art of establishing authentic business relationships built on trust, respect, and shared values.
You'll learn about communication, listening, and making a positive impression.
We'll also cover the significance of transparency and ethical conduct in all your interactions.

Leveraging Mentorship and Support

Mentorship strongly impacts an entrepreneur's journey.

We'll discover how to find mentors and use their advice to overcome obstacles, make smart choices, and enhance your development.

Moreover, we'll explore the significance of support in the entrepreneurial community.

Develop a supportive network of mentors, advisors, and peers for valuable guidance and help.

CHAPTER 12:

TRACKING ACHIEVEMENTS AND ESTABLISHING FRESH OBJECTIVES

Creating Your Own Definition of Success

Define personal success as an entrepreneur to ensure clarity and alignment.

Here, we'll delve into defining personal success. We'll explore the significance of matching your entrepreneurial journey with your values, ambitions, and lifestyle targets.

You'll discover how to create a meaningful definition of success that directs your path.

Entrepreneurial KPIs

You require KPIs to assess your progress and make informed decisions.
We will cover the key performance indicators (KPIs) pertinent to entrepreneurs, such as financial metrics, customer acquisition, and product/service performance.
Learn how to effectively track and analyze KPIs for success in your entrepreneurial goals.

Establishing and Attaining Fresh Objectives

Goals are the blueprint to your desired success.
We'll focus on tactics to reach and surpass new milestones in your entrepreneurial journey.

You'll discover the process of developing SMART goals, dividing them into actionable steps, and maintaining motivation.

Attaining milestones not only gauges success but also drives you towards greater accomplishments.

CHAPTER 13:

CONTINUING AND DEVELOPING YOUR ENTREPRENEURIAL JOURNEY

Achieving Long-Term Sustainability

Entrepreneurship is dependent on sustainability. Here, we'll discuss ways to attain lasting sustainability in your business.

You will acquire skills in establishing a solid base, optimizing resource utilization, and adjusting to dynamic market circumstances.

We'll also cover ethical and environmentally conscious business practices in your sustainability journey.

Embracing Innovation and Evolution

Entrepreneurship centers around innovation and adaptability.
We'll explore how innovation sustains and evolves your business.
Uncover methods to cultivate an innovative culture, spot chances for growth, and outmaneuver competitors.
Success in entrepreneurship hinges on embracing change and actively seeking evolution.

The Ongoing Entrepreneurial Adventure

Entrepreneurship is a continuous journey, not a final destination.

We'll explore the ever-changing entrepreneurial journey and how to embrace it with curiosity and enthusiasm.

Discover motivation, find new opportunities, and feel fulfilled as you grow as an entrepreneur.

We will also discuss the significance of giving back and contributing to the entrepreneurial community.

Keep in mind that your entrepreneurial journey is an incredible adventure, encompassing opportunities, challenges, and personal development, as you dive into this last chapter.

Sustainability, innovation, and curiosity ensure readiness for the entrepreneurial adventure.

CONCLUSION:

YOUR ENTREPRENEURIAL LEGACY

Reflecting on Your Journey

Before completing the transition from employee to entrepreneur, reflect on your journey.
Here, we'll assist you in reflecting on your growth, accomplishments, and the obstacles you've conquered.
Reflecting is crucial for recognizing personal growth and progress.

Encouragement and Final Thoughts

Starting a business takes guts and determination.
We'll inspire you with encouraging words as you pursue your entrepreneurial journey.
You'll discover inspiration to approach each day with excitement and confront fresh obstacles with assurance.

The Entrepreneur's Lasting Legacy

Every entrepreneur's legacy reflects their values, contributions, and impact on the world.
Next, we will discuss the entrepreneurial legacy.
Reflect on the legacy you aim for - innovation, social impact, and inspiring future entrepreneurs.
Your legacy will forever inspire and impact others.

Your entrepreneurial journey is a beginning, not an endpoint.

Your legacy encompasses both your bequest and the influence on future generations.

May your entrepreneurial legacy be characterized by innovation, resilience, and positive change.

www.ingramcontent.com/pod-product-compliance
Lightning Source LLC
Chambersburg PA
CBHW062304290526
45794CB00006B/2692